DATE DUE

Demco, Inc. 38-293

21 NORTH MAIN STREET
TERRYVILLE, CT 06786

DISCOVERING THE CARIBBEAN
History, Politics, and Culture

HAITI

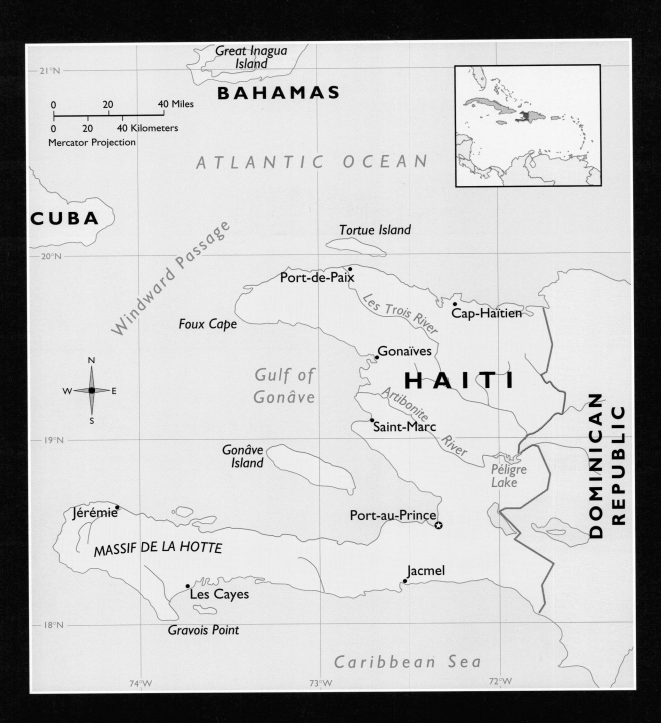

DISCOVERING THE CARIBBEAN
History, Politics, and Culture

HAITI

Bob Temple

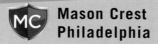

Mason Crest
Philadelphia

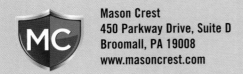

Mason Crest
450 Parkway Drive, Suite D
Broomall, PA 19008
www.masoncrest.com

©2016 by Mason Crest, an imprint of National Highlights, Inc.

Printed and bound in the United States of America.

CPSIA Compliance Information: Batch #DC2015.
For further information, contact Mason Crest at 1-866-MCP-Book.

First printing
1 3 5 7 9 8 6 4 2

Library of Congress Cataloging-in-Publication Data
on file at the Library of Congress

ISBN: 978-1-4222-3312-2 (hc)
ISBN: 978-1-4222-8629-6 (ebook)

Discovering the Caribbean: History, Politics, and Culture series ISBN: 978-1-4222-3307-8

DISCOVERING THE CARIBBEAN: History, Politics, and Culture

Bahamas	Cuba	Leeward Islands
Barbados	Dominican Republic	Puerto Rico
Caribbean Islands:	Haiti	Trinidad & Tobago
Facts & Figures	Jamaica	Windward Islands

TABLE OF CONTENTS

Introduction: Discovering the Caribbean 6

Rugged Beauty and Environmental Devastation 9

A Troubled History 17

Underdeveloped Economy, Grinding Poverty 27

African Influences: The Culture and People 35

Haiti's Cities 45

A Calendar of Haitian Festivals 50

Recipes 52

Series Glossary 54

Project and Report Ideas 56

Chronology 58

Further Reading/Internet Resources 60

For More Information 61

Index 62

KEY ICONS TO LOOK FOR:

Words to Understand: These words with their easy-to-understand definitions will increase the reader's understanding of the text, while building vocabulary skills.

Sidebars: This boxed material within the main text allows readers to build knowledge, gain insights, explore possibilities, and broaden their perspectives by weaving together additional information to provide realistic and holistic perspectives.

Research Projects: Readers are pointed toward areas of further inquiry connected to each chapter. Suggestions are provided for projects that encourage deeper research and analysis.

Text-Dependent Questions: These questions send the reader back to the text for more careful attention to the evidence presented there.

Series Glossary of Key Terms: This back-of-the book glossary contains terminology used throughout this series. Words found here increase the reader's ability to read and comprehend higher-level books and articles in this field.

DISCOVERING THE CARIBBEAN

James D. Henderson

THE CARIBBEAN REGION is a lovely, ethnically diverse part of tropical America. It is at once a sea, rivaling the Mediterranean in size; and it is islands, dozens of them, stretching along the sea's northern and eastern edges. Waters of the Caribbean Sea bathe the eastern shores of Central America's seven nations, as well as those of the South American countries Colombia, Venezuela, and Guyana. The Caribbean islands rise, like a string of pearls, from its warm azure waters. Their sandy beaches, swaying palm trees, and balmy weather give them the aspect of tropical paradises, intoxicating places where time seems to stop.

But it is the people of the Caribbean region who make it a unique place. In their ethnic diversity they reflect their homeland's character as a crossroads of the world for more than five centuries. Africa's imprint is most visible in peoples of the Caribbean, but so too is that of Europe. South and East Asian strains enrich the Caribbean ethnic mosaic as well. Some islanders reveal traces of the region's first inhabitants, the Carib and Taino Indians, who flourished there when Columbus appeared among them in 1492.

Though its sparkling waters and inviting beaches beckon tourists from around the globe, the Caribbean islands provide a significant portion of the world's sugar, bananas, coffee, cacao, and natural fibers. They are strategically important also, for they guard the Panama Canal's eastern approaches.

The Caribbean possesses a cultural diversity rivaling the ethnic kaleidoscope that is its human population. Though its dominant culture is Latin American, defined by languages and customs bequeathed it by Spain and France, significant parts of the Caribbean bear the cultural imprint of

A man and his pack animal on the road to Lake Saumatre.

Northwestern Europe: Denmark, the Netherlands, and most significantly, Britain.

So welcome to the Caribbean! These lavishly illustrated books survey the human and physical geography of the Caribbean, along with its economic and historical development. Geared to the needs of students and teachers, each of the eleven volumes in the series contains a glossary of terms, a chronology, and ideas for class reports. And each volume contains a recipe section featuring tasty, easy-to-prepare dishes popular in the countries dealt with. Each volume is indexed, and contains a bibliography featuring web sources for further information.

Whether old or young, readers of the eleven-volume series Discovering the Caribbean will come away with a new appreciation of this tropical sea, its jewel-like islands, and its fascinating and friendly people!

(Opposite) Haiti's presidential palace was just one of thousands of buildings destroyed when a powerful earthquake struck the capital, Port-au-Prince, in January 2010. (Right) Farm fields cover the hillsides of rural Haiti. Many people in the country live off whatever crops they are able to grow. Haiti is one of the poorest countries in the world.

1 RUGGED BEAUTY AND ENVIRONMENTAL DEVASTATION

A LITTLE LESS THAN 600 miles (966 kilometers) southeast of the southern tip of Florida lies an island called Hispaniola. This island, along with Cuba, Jamaica, and Puerto Rico, makes up an island chain known as the *Greater Antilles*, which is one of three island groups in the *West Indies*.

Christopher Columbus discovered Hispaniola, and gave the island its name, in 1492. One legend says that when Columbus returned to Spain, he tried to illustrate the island's landscape for the king and queen by crumpling up a piece of paper. When he uncrumpled the paper, the bumps and ridges demonstrated the island's rugged terrain.

Columbus was struck by the beauty of Hispaniola. More than 500 years later, however, much of the island has been ravaged by environmentally destructive human activity. Today, two countries share Hispaniola. The Dominican Republic occupies the eastern two-thirds of the island. The western third is Haiti.

Haiti covers 10,714 square miles (27,750 sq km), making it a little smaller than the state of Maryland. It occupies an important geographic location. The body of water between it and Cuba, called the Windward Passage, has long been an important route for ships. It is one of the main routes linking Central America with Europe and other parts of the world.

The northern and southern parts of Haiti are made up of rugged mountain ranges that stretch west toward Cuba. They form a pair of *peninsulas*

Words to Understand in This Chapter

cultivate—to use land to grow crops.

deforestation—the destruction of forests through the massive cutting of trees.

erosion—a natural process in which unprotected soil is carried away by water or wind.

Greater Antilles—an island chain that includes Cuba, Hispaniola, Jamaica, and Puerto Rico.

habitat—the place or area where a plant or animal naturally lives.

hurricane—a strong storm featuring winds as high as 150 miles (241 km) per hour, heavy rainfall, and, frequently, dangerous lightning.

peninsula—an area of land that is surrounded on three sides by water.

reserves—areas of land that are set aside and managed by government agencies to help preserve plants and animals in their natural environments.

West Indies—an area in the Caribbean made up of three different island chains: the Greater Antilles, the Lesser Antilles, and the Bahamas.

A view of La Plaine du Cul-de-Sac, near Port-au-Prince at the base of Haiti's mountainous southern peninsula.

and give the country the appearance of a large horseshoe. The northern peninsula extends into the Atlantic Ocean about 100 miles (161 km). The southern peninsula is twice as long and reaches into the Caribbean Sea. In between lies the Gulf of Gonâve. Within the gulf is an island, Isle de la Gonâve, which is part of Haiti. At the center of the "horseshoe," between the two peninsulas, sits Port-au-Prince, the capital city.

Haiti is one of the most mountainous countries in the world. In fact, more than 75 percent of Haiti's land area is made up of mountain ranges, ridges, and cliffs. Four large mountain ranges—two in the north and two in the south—make traveling through the country difficult. The Massif du Nord stretches from the northern peninsula southeast and across the border into the Dominican Republic. The Montagnes Noires range is just to its south. In the far southeast of the country lies the Massif de la Selle range, while the Massif de la Hotte range stretches westward into the southern peninsula.

Between the mountain ranges are vast, fertile valleys and a few large lakes. The Central Plain, which lies between the two northern mountain ranges, and the North Plain, located along the country's northern coastline, boast rich soil.

In Haiti, any land that is remotely suited to farming has been *cultivated*. Because a relatively small percentage of the land is flat, Haitians farm even the steep mountain slopes. In some cases, farmers suspend themselves from ropes, risking injury in order to cultivate the land.

Unfortunately, much of the good land has been overfarmed, and even areas that aren't suitable for farming have been tilled. As a result, Haiti has faced terrible soil *erosion*. What remains is land that is less productive, thus creating a cycle that contributes to the country's poverty.

Dozens of rivers and streams flow out of the mountains and through Haiti. The Artibonite River, the country's longest, rises in the Dominican Republic and flows from the far eastern portion of Haiti to the west, where it empties into the Gulf of Gonâve.

Haiti was once home to large tracts of forest, but most of those have been cut down. *Deforestation* in the country continues to this day, as remaining forests are being cleared to create more farmland and to provide fuel.

While much of Haiti is difficult to traverse, and other parts have been overused, Haiti is also a land of great beauty. Tree-covered hills, breathtaking mountain ranges, gorgeous waterfalls, and beautiful plants are the highlights of Haiti's landscape.

Quick Facts: The Geography of Haiti

Location: in the West Indies, on the western third of the island of Hispaniola, which is between Puerto Rico and Cuba in the Caribbean Sea

Area: (slightly smaller than Maryland)
 total: 10,714 square miles (27,750 sq km)
 land: 10,641 square miles (27,560 sq km)
 water: 73 square miles (190 sq km)

Borders: Dominican Republic, 171 miles (275 km)

Climate: tropical; semiarid where mountains in the east cut off the trade winds

Terrain: mostly rough and mountainous

Elevation extremes:
 lowest point: Caribbean Sea—0 feet
 highest point: Chaine de la Selle—8,793 feet (2,680 meters)

Natural hazards: hurricanes, floods, mud slides, occasional earthquakes

Source: Adapted from CIA World Factbook 2015.

CLIMATE

Because of its location near the equator, Haiti has a tropical climate—warm temperatures, high humidity, and abundant rainfall. Temperatures in lowland areas range from 70°F to 95°F (21°C to 35°C), and even in the mountains it rarely drops below 50°F (10°C).

Up to 80 inches (203 centimeters) of rain falls annually in the tropical forests of the northern mountains. The southern coast gets an average of about 40 inches (102 cm) of rain per year.

As in the United States, July and August are the hottest months in Haiti. In the lowland areas, mountains prevent cool breezes from moderating temperatures during this time of year. The capital city, Port-au-Prince, is one of the hottest major cities in the world because the mountains that surround it block the breezes. Many wealthier Haitians live on higher ground, where temperatures are somewhat cooler.

From May through November, rainfall is copious. Showers can be sudden, often arriving in the late afternoon. From December through March, however, Haiti is mostly dry and temperatures are more moderate.

August and September are dangerous months in Haiti—*hurricane* season. These fierce storms, carrying winds as high as 150 miles (241 km) per hour, drop huge amounts of rain and can flatten buildings and trees. In 1963, Hurricane Flora killed more than 2,500 Haitians. As the storm blew into the island, toppling homes and buildings, the massive rainfall caused mudslides down the mountains. Many of the dead were buried in the mud. In 1998, Hurricane Georges left more than 160,000 Haitians homeless.

PLANTS AND ANIMALS

The overuse of Haiti's land for farming and the removal of most of its forests have caused the elimination of some species of plant and animal life. When Columbus arrived in Hispaniola, he found vast forests of pine, oak, redwood, and mahogany; banana groves; plains full of cacti and grasses; and marshes of wild ginger. Today, Haiti's woodland region is almost entirely gone. Few countries in the world have experienced environmental devastation as severe.

Hardwood trees now grow only on the highest reaches of Haiti's peaks. But fruit trees—including oranges, cherries, and avocados—can still be found. Flowering shrubs such as orchids also lend beauty to the land.

Deforestation has claimed the *habitat* of numerous birds, including flamingos, falcons, and spotted sandpipers. Haiti remains home to a variety of reptile and insect species, however. These include crocodiles, snakes, lizards, scorpions, and spiders. In recent years Haiti has established nature *reserves* to protect its plant and animal life, particularly endangered and threatened species. It is hoped that these reserves will also teach people the value of preserving the land, and that they will be inspired to help restore the country's natural environment.

2010 EARTHQUAKE

On January 12, 2010, Haiti was struck by an earthquake measuring 7.0 on the Richter scale. It was the country's most severe earthquake in over 200 years, and was followed by dozens of smaller quakes, called aftershocks, over the next several weeks. The quake destroyed much of Haiti's capital, Port-au-Prince, as well as many smaller towns and villages. The government estimated that more than 150,000 people had died as a result of the earthquake, and a million Haitians had lost their homes. Many countries, including the United States and Canada, sent food, medicine, and rescue workers to help with the crisis. Additional foreign aid was sent to help rebuild Haiti's infrastructure over the next several years.

TEXT-DEPENDENT QUESTIONS

1. What is the body of water between Haiti and Cuba called? Why is it important?
2. What percentage of Haiti's land area is made up of mountain ranges, ridges, and cliffs?
3. Which months are considered hurricane season in Haiti?

(Opposite), In December 1990, Haitians took to the streets to celebrate the election of Jean-Bertrand Aristide. However, Aristide's election was soon undone by a military coup d'état. (Right) Michel Martelly was elected president of Haiti in 2011.

2 A Troubled History

HISTORY PROCLAIMS THAT Christopher Columbus discovered the West Indies, including the island of Hispaniola (which now includes Haiti and the Dominican Republic), in 1492. But for thousands of years before Columbus arrived, the land was inhabited by *indigenous* tribes.

In fact, American Indians may have lived on the island between 5,000 and 7,000 years ago. These ancient natives lived off the land as hunter-gatherers. By the late 15th century, a tribe called the Arawak inhabited the island, which they called Ayiti.

The first European settlement on Hispaniola occurred by accident. On December 25, 1492, one of Columbus's three ships, the *Santa María*, ran aground near the present-day city of Cap-Haïtien, Haiti. Because his men could not all fit on the remaining two ships, Columbus ordered that timbers from the *Santa María* be used to build a fort. Of the original 85 to 90 members of the expedition, about 40 stayed behind at the stockade, which Columbus called La Navidad ("Christmas" in Spanish).

When Columbus returned to Europe in early 1493, he was hailed as a hero. He quickly assembled a much larger expedition consisting of 17 ships and about 1,500 men. When the members of the second expedition arrived in Hispaniola, however, they discovered that La Navidad had been destroyed. The men who had stayed behind were probably killed by the Arawaks.

Columbus put his brother Bartholomew in charge of building another settlement. Over the next four decades, the Europeans killed or enslaved the native population of the island.

THE COLONIAL YEARS

After the discovery of gold in the area that is now the Dominican Republic, Spanish settlers flocked to the island of Hispaniola. The enslaved Indian population was forced to mine for gold and grow food. By the 1530s, the Indian

Words to Understand in This Chapter

buccaneer—a pirate who raided passing ships to steal their cargo.
colony—an area of land ruled by a distant country.
dictator—a leader who holds sole power in a country and frequently rules in a brutal fashion.
indigenous—native or original to a particular area.
plantation—a large tract of agricultural land, especially one worked by slaves.

population had been reduced to a few hundred, so the Spanish settlers imported African slaves to perform their work.

The Spaniards also spread their influence to other islands in the Caribbean as well as Central and South America. Spanish settlements in places such as Cuba, Mexico, and Peru offered a greater opportunity for riches, and Hispaniola soon became somewhat of a backwater. The Spaniards who remained on the island moved into a settlement in what is now the Dominican Republic, on the eastern two-thirds of Hispaniola. They called their settlement Santo Domingo.

On the western third of the island—the region that is now Haiti—French settlers found a home. The French, along with Dutch and English settlers, soon controlled the northern and western coasts of Hispaniola. They also took over a small island off the northern coast called Tortue. Spanish ships loaded with gold and other riches often passed near this island on their way back to Spain. And *buccaneers* based in Tortue or on the northern coast of Hispaniola often sailed out to plunder these treasure ships.

By the end of the 17th century, Spain had lost interest in the western third of Hispaniola. In 1697 this land was officially given to France as part of the Treaty of Ryswick. The area, called Saint Domingue, became a French *colony*. The colonists established large coffee *plantations* and imported more African slaves to work the fields. Other crops included indigo, which produces a valuable blue dye, and sugarcane.

The Saint Domingue colony had a fixed social structure. At the top were the white plantation owners, who lived a life of luxury. Below the white colonists were the mulattoes, or *affranchis*. These were people of mixed racial heritage (often French and African) who had been granted French citizenship. Some of them owned plantations, but they were not considered the equals of the white plantation owners. At the bottom of the social ladder were the slaves. By the late 1700s, Saint Domingue was home to more than 500,000 slaves—over eight times the number of colonists. This huge majority soon presented a difficult problem.

In 1789 the French Revolution broke out. Among its stated goals were liberty and equality for all French people, and as news of the Revolution spread to Saint Domingue, *affranchis* and slaves began to question their second-class status. In 1791, *affranchis* in Saint Domingue rose up against the white minority. The revolt grew quickly as slaves led by a man named Toussaint-Louverture also rose up. The French government of Saint Domingue was quickly overthrown, and Toussaint-Louverture took power. Four years later, the Spanish gave control of the remainder of the island to the French, but Toussaint-Louverture conquered that territory as well. In the process, he set free all of the slaves on Hispaniola.

In 1802, the French emperor Napoleon Bonaparte dispatched an army of 25,000 men to restore Saint Domingue as a French colony. The more powerful French army won early victories over the rebel forces, and Toussaint-Louverture was captured and sent to France, where he died in prison. However, disease would soon take a huge toll on the French soldiers. Yellow fever killed many and weakened those who remained. In 1803, the rebels reclaimed the land. Their leader, General Jean-Jacques Dessalines, declared it a free and independent country on January 1, 1804. He called the new nation Haiti and declared himself emperor.

Years of Unrest

Stability did not follow independence. In fact, Haiti experienced even more turmoil after throwing off its French colonial master. Dessalines was assassinated in 1806, and two other generals battled for control of the country. Alexandre Pétion ruled the southern portion of Haiti, while Henri Christophe established himself as king of the north. In time a man named Jean-Pierre Boyer took Pétion's place in the south in 1818. After the death of Christophe in 1820, Boyer reunified Haiti. A year later, Boyer moved to take control of the eastern portion of Hispaniola (which the Spanish had retaken in 1809).

Haiti ruled the entire island until 1844. That year a revolt once again split off the eastern two-thirds, which was renamed the Dominican Republic.

Over the next 70 years, 32 different men ruled Haiti. During this time, the country faced serious problems at home and abroad. Unrest spread among the Haitian people, and the country's international debts were left unpaid.

By the outbreak of World War I, the government of the United States had become worried about having such an unstable land so close to its borders. In 1915, as part of an agreement with the Haitian government, President Woodrow Wilson sent U.S. troops to Haiti.

The American troops helped restore order in the country and aided in a number of other ways. They implemented a sanitation program that helped eliminate yellow fever. They also constructed roads, buildings, and schools. But the Haitian people didn't want Americans controlling their fate. In 1934, the American troops left. The result was another long period of unrest in Haiti.

PAPA AND BABY DOC

François "Papa Doc" Duvalier (1907–1971) used his secret police to terrorize and destroy his political opponents.

In 1957, Haitians rejoiced as François "Papa Doc" Duvalier, a much admired country doctor, was elected president. In the ensuing years, however, Duvalier became a *dictator*. He ordered the imprisonment or killing of his political enemies. In 1964 he declared himself president for life. Duvalier even had Haiti's constitution amended to allow him to appoint his successor. He chose his son, Jean-Claude.

Following his father's death in 1971, Jean-Claude Duvalier, only 19 years old at the time, took power. With the country's army and secret police forces at his disposal, the younger Duvalier, nicknamed "Baby Doc," also ruled as a dictator. The secret police, known as the Tontons Macoutes, were particularly feared by the Haitian people. Meanwhile, the country fell deeper and deeper into poverty.

In 1986, a revolt finally forced Duvalier to leave the country. An army general named Henri Namphy took control, but he was unable to rein in the Tontons Macoutes. Although a new constitution was adopted in March 1987, attacks on polling places and voters forced the postponement of elections scheduled for November. And, when a civilian president was finally elected in January 1988, General Namphy quickly overthrew the new government and regained power.

Later in the year, Namphy was overthrown and General Prosper Avril declared himself president. He, too, ruled as a dictator until his resignation in 1990.

Aristide and Democracy

In December 1990 Jean-Bertrand Aristide, a former Catholic priest, was elected president. Though popular among Haiti's poor, Aristide was overthrown and forced into exile by the military in 1991. The Organization of American States and the United Nations imposed economic sanctions on Haiti in an attempt to force the nation's military rulers to permit Aristide's return to power. Though Haiti's already bleak economic situation quickly deteriorated, the generals resisted. Frightened by the continued unrest, and with little hope of escaping the grinding poverty in their homeland, many Haitians attempted the dangerous sea crossing to the United States in whatever small craft they could make or find. The U.S. Coast Guard intercepted thousands of these would-be immigrants, most of whom were eventually returned to Haiti.

In July 1994, the United Nations Security Council authorized the invasion of Haiti by a multinational force. On September 18, with U.S. invasion troops already airborne, Haiti's ruling generals finally backed down. With American soldiers in the country to ensure order, Aristide returned to Haiti and resumed his presidency on October 15, serving the remainder of his term. In 1995, René Préval was elected president.

In March 1995, United Nations peacekeeping troops took over from the American force. The U.N. peacekeepers remained until January 2000, at which time Haiti was again left to rule itself.

U.N. peacekeepers fire rubber bullets and tear gas toward demonstrators in Port-au-Prince, April 2008. Haitians rioted in the spring of 2008 because of the high price of food.

CONTINUED TURMOIL

In national elections held in 2000, Jean-Bertrand Aristide was once again voted into the president's office. Opposition parties boycotted the election, so Aristide won about 90 percent of the vote. His Lavalas Family Party also won large majorities in Haiti's two-chamber legislature. However, complaints of voting fraud were widespread.

In December 2001, armed commandos stormed Haiti's National Palace in an attempt to seize control of the government. The coup d'état failed after a fierce battle between the attackers, who were believed to have connections to Haiti's armed forces, and police and army units loyal to Aristide.

But the political situation in the country worsened. In the weeks and months following the unsuccessful coup, armed gangs of Aristide supporters attacked, intimidated, and sometimes murdered government critics, journalists, and opposition politicians. Many observers believed that these gangs acted with the approval of—and perhaps even under direction from—the ruling Lavalas Family Party.

In early 2004, a bloody revolt forced Aristide to go into exile in February 2004. A multinational peacekeeping force was sent by the United Nations to stabilize the country. In 2006, René Préval was reelected as Haiti's president.

In November 2014, Cap-Haïtien and other cities in northern Haiti suffered serious flooding, leaving more than 12 people dead and thousands homeless.

However, Haiti remained troubled by political instability, economic problems, and violent clashes between rival groups struggling for power. Michel Martelly took over as president of Haiti in May 2011, but his administration has made little headway with Haiti's many problems. Anti-government protests erupted throughout the country during 2014 and 2015.

TEXT-DEPENDENT QUESTIONS

1. What 1697 treaty granted France control over the western one-third of Hispaniola?
2. What former priest turned politician was forced into exile by the military in 1991?

(Opposite) Haitian men saw fresh timber into boards near Port-au-Prince. Today, less than 1 percent of Haiti has tree cover. This widespread deforestation has hastened massive soil erosion and increased land slides and flash flooding. (Right) A woman sorts raw coffee beans in Jacmel. Farming remains an important part of Haiti's economy.

3 UNDERDEVELOPED ECONOMY, GRINDING POVERTY

WHEN HAITI WAS a French colony, it produced vast quantities of agricultural products, particularly sugar. But the country's political leaders and wealthy plantation owners benefited most during that time. As a result, much of the country lived in poverty, and the economy of Haiti was almost always unstable.

Today, Haiti's days as a rich, lush land are long gone. The land has deteriorated from overfarming, and government instability has resulted in political and social unrest. Haiti has become one of the poorest countries in the world. Even when financial aid flowed into the country from foreign lands, it was often misused to benefit political leaders and the wealthy, instead of serving the general population for which it was intended.

Today Haiti is the poorest country in the Western Hemisphere. According to recent statistics, approximately 80 percent of the country's population of nearly 10 million lives below the poverty line, with 54 percent living in abject poverty (defined as earning less than $1.25 a day). About 41 percent of Haitians are unemployed, and more than two-thirds of Haiti's labor force does not have formal jobs.

ECONOMIC OVERVIEW

Statistics hint at just how dismal Haiti's economic situation is. The World Bank, a development-assistance organization, reported Haiti's 2014 *gross domestic product (GDP)*—the total value of goods and services the country produced that year—at just $18.5 billion. In overall size, Haiti's economy ranked 145th among the world's nations. In 2014 Haiti's neighbor on the island of Hispaniola, the Dominican Republic, ranked 74th overall with a GDP of $135.7 billion—more than seven times larger than Haiti's.

Words to Understand in This Chapter

gross domestic product (GDP)—the total value of goods and services produced in a country in a one-year period.
remittances—an amount of money, often sent by mail or by bank transfer, from a foreign worker to family members in his or her native country.
subsistence farming—the cultivation of a usually quite small tract of land for the purpose of feeding one's own family.

A woman prepares "clay cakes"—sun-baked disks made from mud, butter, and salt, which are sold in markets for about 10 US cents each. These clay cakes, which many Haitians must consume to ease their hunger, have become a symbol of Haiti's struggle with extreme poverty.

For the average Haitian, abject poverty is the rule. In 2014, the World Bank estimated that GDP per capita (basically a measure of each person's share of the national economy) among Haitians was just $1,800. In the Western Hemisphere, the next poorest countries are Honduras and Nicaragua. Their 2014 GDP per capita ($4,800 for Nicaragua; $4,700 for Honduras) was nearly three times as high as Haiti's. The GDP per capita of citizens of the Dominican Republic ($12,800) is more than seven times higher than those of their Haitian neighbors.

A NATION OF FARMERS

Agriculture is the largest component of the Haitian economy. Farm products make up 25 percent of the country's GDP. Almost 40 percent of all Haitians are involved in agriculture in some way. But most of the country's crops are grown on very small farms that barely support an individual family. *Subsistence farming*—the growing of food to provide for one's own family, with no surplus—makes up a large share of agricultural activity in Haiti.

When the country achieved its independence, many of the larger plantations were divided up into smaller tracts that were given to freed slaves. These farms, often called "peasant farms," are barely big enough to support a single family; the average Haitian farmer owns less than two acres (0.8 hectares) of land. Moreover, modern agricultural machinery is very rare.

Of the few crops that Haiti exports, coffee is the most prominent. Haiti's mountainous regions provide a fertile setting for coffee growing. However, Haiti isn't a world leader in coffee production. It can't come close to matching the output of other countries in Latin and South America. Sugarcane production, once a staple of the Haitian economy, has also declined. Today, mangoes, rice, cocoa, and oils round out Haiti's meager agricultural exports.

INDUSTRY AND FOREIGN AID

In the 1970s, dictator François Duvalier tried to lure foreign businesses to Haiti. Because Haiti's people were so poor and the country's underdeveloped economy made finding jobs difficult, Haitian workers would accept very low wages in factories that produced items such as clothing. Plus, there were no unions to protect workers' rights in Haiti. In the 1980s, legislation in the United States made it economical for American-owned businesses to establish facilities to make sporting goods, toys, and other products in Haiti. Today, textiles and clothing account for about 90 percent of Haiti's exports.

Haiti has long functioned with the help of financial aid from the United

Quick Facts: The Economy of Haiti

Gross domestic product (GDP*):
$18.54 billion
GDP per capita: $1,800
Inflation: 4.3%
Natural resources: bauxite, copper, calcium carbonate, gold, marble, hydropower, arable land.
Agriculture (24.7% of GDP): coffee, mangoes, cocoa, sugarcane, rice, corn, sorghum; wood, vetiver.
Services (55.3% of GDP): tourism, banking, government.
Industry (20% of GDP): textiles, sugar refining, flour milling, cement, light assembly using imported parts.
Foreign trade (2014):
Exports: $903.1 million: apparel, manufactures, oils, cocoa, mangoes, coffee.
Imports: $3.458 billion: food, manufactured goods, machinery and transport equipment, fuels, raw materials.
Currency exchange rate: 47.22 gourdes = U.S. $1 (2015).

*GDP = the total value of goods and services produced in one year.
Figures are 2014 estimates unless otherwise indicated. Sources: CIA World Factbook 2015.

States and other countries. In 2008, the U.S. government passed the Haitian Hemispheric Opportunity through Partnership Encouragement Act. Known as HOPE II, this legislation helped to increase Haiti's apparel exports and promote foreign investment in the country by eliminating taxes and tariffs on some goods imported to the United States. In 2010, the US. Congress voted to extend HOPE II until 2020.

Haiti's government owed significant money to foreign nations, but after the 2010 earthquake many countries forgave Haiti's debt. Despite this, the country's debt had once again risen to over $1.5 billion by early 2015.

During the presidency of René Préval (2006-2011), Haiti forged an economic partnership with Venezuela. In 2007, that oil-rich South American

A seamstress sews a garment in a factory at the Sonapi industrial park near Port-au-Prince.

country announced that it would build four new power plants as well as an oil refinery in Haiti. Venezuela and Cuba also offered to invest up to a billion dollars in Haiti.

Since 2011, the administration of Michel Martelly has attempted to attract more foreign investment into Haiti, in order to encourage industrial development. However, investment in Haiti remains limited, in large part due to poor infrastructure and limited access to electrical power.

OTHER INDUSTRIES

For a long time, Haiti—unlike many other Caribbean nations—failed to benefit from tourism. The country's political instability and awful health conditions made most people wary of traveling there. While tourism in Haiti has increased in recent years, the country still lags far behind other Caribbean nations as a destination for travelers.

About half of Haiti's workforce is involved in the service sector—operating shops in local markets, working as servants in the homes of the wealthy, or performing jobs in the tourist industry, for example. Only about 12 percent of the workforce is employed in industrial production; agriculture employs about 40 percent of the workforce.

The barter system is an important part of the Haitian economy. Many farmers don't have cash to pay for necessities such as clothing. So they trade some of the food they grow with people who have other goods. This way they can continue to get the things they need without using money.

Due to the poor economic conditions, many Haitians must move to other countries, such as the Dominican Republic or the United States, to find work. *Remittances*, or money that these workers send home to their families each month, represents a significant source of national income. Haitians working in other countries sent home a total of more than $2 billion in 2014—more than the total value of Haiti's exports that year.

THE FUTURE

Numerous problems hang over the heads of the Haitian people. Because so much of the country's economy depends on agriculture, the land is critical. But that land has been severely overused, and in many areas the soil is no longer as productive as it once was. Soil erosion has also left large tracts unsuitable for any farming. And as the population of the country continues to grow, the small country will have even more trouble supporting its people.

TEXT-DEPENDENT QUESTIONS

1. What percentage of Haitians live below the poverty level?
2. What is the most prominent crop exported from Haiti?

(Opposite) A woman lifts a large fish at a seafood stand. (Right) A teacher questions a child during class in a school in Cite Soleil, a slum of Port-au-Prince. Although education is free, few poor Haitians are able to take advantage.

4 AFRICAN INFLUENCES: THE CULTURE AND PEOPLE

THE VAST MAJORITY of Haitian people today are descendants of the African slaves brought to the land by Spanish settlers. Roughly 95 percent of the nearly 10 million people who live in Haiti are black, with the remaining 5 percent divided between whites and people of mixed European and African heritage, known as mulattoes.

Because of the relatively small land area that Haiti encompasses, its population density is one of the highest in the world: more than 907 people per square mile (350 per square kilometer). And because the nation's many mountainous areas are much more sparsely populated, Haiti's lowland and urban areas are even more crowded that that figure would indicate. While poverty limits the lives of many, Haitians have rich traditions and culture.

EDUCATION

It isn't surprising that a country as poor as Haiti would have an undereducated population. Public schools are free and open to boys and girls, and private education is available for some children through religious groups like the Roman Catholic Church, but a large percentage of Haiti's children don't attend school. School attendance isn't required, and many families can't afford textbooks or other school supplies. While most children receive some elementary education, by the age of 10 or 11—when secondary education begins in Haiti—only about 10 percent are still in school.

Secondary school is very rigorous, lasting as long as seven years, and

Words to Understand in This Chapter

Black Consciousness movement—a movement of the 1970s stressing Africa's contribution to world culture.

HIV—the virus that causes AIDS, a deadly disease marked by a weakened immune system.

literate—able to read and write.

loas—African and Haitian deities called upon during a vodun ceremony.

Négritude—a Black Consciousness movement founded in Paris in the 1930s by poet Aimé Césaire.

possession—the moment in a vodun ceremony when the loa takes control of the body and mind of the worshipper.

vodun (voodoo)—a Haitian religion that is a mixture of African beliefs, based on ancestral superstitions and traditions.

students must pass a national exam before they can graduate. Vocational schools help train young people to enter the workforce. Those who make it through high school and wish to continue their education have only one choice within the country—the University of Haiti. Children of the wealthy class usually leave Haiti to study abroad.

Recent data indicates that less than half of Haitians over the age of 15 are *literate*. Factoring in the size of the under-15 population group (about 34 percent of Haiti's population), as few as three in ten Haitians may be able to read and write.

HEALTH

Widespread health problems plague Haiti. Sanitary conditions are generally poor in both rural and urban areas. Nearly three-quarters of Haitian homes lack running water, and water supplies are often unsafe. For example, streams that run near a town are often used for drinking water and for washing clothes, but they might also carry sewage away.

In addition, Haiti has a shortage of doctors and hospitals. And where there are hospitals, they often lack supplies and medications. Adding to these basic problems is the prevalence of *HIV*, the virus that causes AIDS. More than 140,000 people, roughly 2 percent of Haiti's population, is infected with the virus, one of the highest rates of infection in the Western Hemisphere. Because of these problems, many babies die in infancy. Haiti's infant mortality rate is more than eight times higher than that of the United States and nearly three times as high as that of the neighboring Dominican Republic. AIDS has also taken a toll on the average life expectancy in Haiti, which is about 63 years. Very few of the country's citizens can afford medications to treat AIDS, which cost six times more than what most Haitians earn in a year.

LANGUAGE

While French and Creole are both official languages of Haiti, Creole is the language of choice among the common people. French is spoken mostly by the wealthy and well educated. Children start out learning Creole in school, but as they progress into high school, they also study French.

Most of the signs in Haiti are printed in Creole, which originated as a way for slaves (who spoke various African languages, depending on their

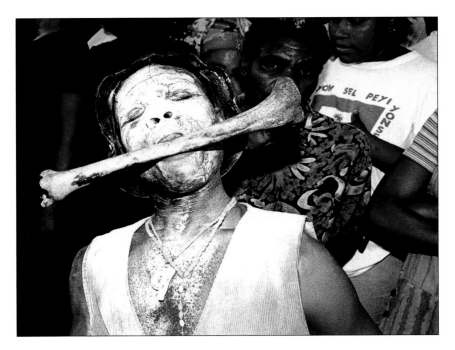

A practitioner of vodun holds a human bone in his mouth while in a trance during a ritual ceremony honoring Guede, the god of the dead. Vodun, or voodoo, is practiced by a large percentage of Haiti's population, who may also practice Christianity.

Quick Facts: The People of Haiti

Population: 9,996,731

Ethnic groups: black 95%, mulatto and white 5%.

Age structure:
0–14 years: 34%
15–64 years: 61.9%
65 years and over: 4.1%

Population growth rate: 1.08%

Birth rate: 22.83 births/1,000 population.

Death rate: 7.91 deaths/1,000 population.

Infant mortality rate: 49.43 deaths/1,000 live births.

Total fertility rate: 2.79 children born per woman.

Life expectancy at birth: 63.18 years
male: 61.77 years
female: 64.6 years

Religions: Roman Catholic 80%, Protestant 16%, none 1%, other 3%. Roughly half of the population practices vodun (voodoo).

Languages: French (official), Creole.

Literacy rate (age 15 and older who can read and write): 48.7% (2006 est.).

Source: CIA World Factbook 2015.

place of origin) to communicate with one another without their masters' knowledge. In the process, Creole evolved from a simplified means of communication (called a pidgin language) into a full language system. Since slaves were actually in the majority, outnumbering their masters many times over, the language quickly grew in popularity. Today 95 percent of Haitians are descendants of slaves, so it's not surprising that Creole is the language spoken by the majority of the population.

French is limited to the upper class and is used in formal meetings and speeches. Because so few Haitians reach high school—when French is first systematically taught—the use of French is almost a sign of status.

RELIGION

Officially, Roman Catholicism is the most popular religion in Haiti. Until 1987, it was the only officially recognized religion in the country. The Spanish explorers who came to Haiti and who eventually colonized it brought Catholicism with them.

Today, Catholicism in Haiti is mixed with—and often overshadowed by—*vodun*, or voodoo. Vodun is practiced by the vast majority of Haitians.

Slaves transported to Haiti during the colonial period brought with them a wide variety of African religious customs and beliefs. Over the years, these became melded into vodun, a mix of beliefs that has no official teachings and is not practiced in a traditional church. Instead, it is based on ancestral traditions. Believers worship spirits, or *loas*. Many *loas* are African deities, though some are of Haitian origin. During

A painting titled *Black Madonna and Child*, from a museum in Port-au-Prince. The Négritude movement emphasizes the importance of African culture and creativity.

vodun ceremonies the *loa* manifests itself in the worshipper through a process called **possession**. Vodun rituals involve music and rhythmic dance, and are designed to attract the attention of the *loa*.

Because some vodun practices often makes Christians uncomfortable, they have often denounced it. Missionaries have tried to convert practitioners of vodun to other religions, mostly without success.

Arts and Culture

Haiti has a rich tradition of art and culture. The slaves brought much of their African culture and art with them, but over the years a uniquely Haitian style has developed.

Poverty and dismal living conditions haven't dampened Haitians' appreciation for the arts. Large murals adorn walls and buildings all around Haiti and are even painted on public buses in the bigger cities. A style of painting called Haitian Primitive has gained international recognition. It features bright colors and elaborate shapes or images of people.

René Depestre was a Haitian poet who won international recognition during the mid-20th century as a member of the **Négritude** movement. *Négritude*, a term invented by Aimé Césaire of Martinique, emphasizes the importance of African culture and black creativity in human history. The poetry of Depestre and Césaire was influential in the **Black Consciousness movement** seen in Latin America, the United States, and Africa during the 1970s.

Dancing and music are important to the people of Haiti. At the heart of all Haitian music is the drum. Drums are often decorated with Haitian paint-

Haitian teenagers play soccer in a Port-Au-Prince slum.

ings, and their beat provides the rhythm for the dances that form such an important part of Haiti's many festivals and celebrations.

Another important part of Haitian culture is storytelling. Children gather around to hear the stories of their elders, and everyone seems to join in to tell favorite tales. Most Haitians don't have access to the modern forms of entertainment Americans enjoy, such as television and movies.

RECREATION AND ENTERTAINMENT

Besides dancing, the favorite recreational activity in Haiti is soccer. Haitians also play baseball, which is extremely popular in the neighboring Dominican Republic. But soccer is the favorite sport of most Haitians, and children can be seen playing it everywhere. If no ball is available, children simply tie some rags into the shape of a ball and play with that. Some Haitians play basketball, too, and long-distance running has become popular as well. Haiti doesn't sponsor national teams for many competitions, and sports aren't played at the professional level as they are in the United States.

Some Haitians enjoy cockfighting, in which trained roosters battle each other, usually to the death. Many people gamble on these events, wagering on which rooster will win the battle. Trainers raise their roosters especially for cockfighting, and the fights take place regularly during the summer months.

TEXT-DEPENDENT QUESTIONS

1. What language is spoken by most Haitians?
2. What is the Négritude movement?

(Opposite) An aerial view of Port-Au-Prince shows the sprawling, crowded capital city. (Right) Cap-Haïtien, in northern Haiti on the Atlantic coast, was founded in 1670 by the French and served as the capital of colonial Haiti for more than a century.

5 Haiti's Cities

HAITI DOESN'T HAVE many large cities, because most of its people are involved in agriculture—the majority, in fact, survive by growing their own food. Living conditions within the cities are often particularly difficult. Many people live in *shantytowns*, with rough tin walls and roofs connecting one shack to another. The large number of people crammed into small areas makes Haitian cities a fertile breeding ground for disease. In such settings proper sanitation is rare.

Port-au-Prince

Haiti's capital city, Port-au-Prince, is located in a bay off the Cul-de-Sac plain in the Gulf of Gonâve. The city was named after one of the first ships to land in the area, the *Prince*, which arrived in 1749 (*Port-au-Prince* is French for

"Port of the Prince"). Port-au-Prince was the capital of Saint Domingue when it was a French colony.

The city has always been the heart of Haiti, although it has undergone a number of transformations. Port-au-Prince, in part or in whole, has been destroyed by floods and hurricanes, damaged by earthquakes, consumed by fires, and scarred in disturbances accompanying the country's many political upheavals.

Today, Port-au-Prince is Haiti's largest city. Within the city limits, the huge *mansions* of political leaders and the wealthy exist nearly side by side with crowded, sprawling slums in which people live beneath corrugated tin roofs. Between 2.3 million and 3 million Haitians live in or around Port-au-Prince.

Port-au-Prince is Haiti's most important seaport as well as its commercial center. It is home to some foreign manufacturing operations and many smaller shops and places of business. Factories create textiles, cement, sporting goods, processed food, and rum.

The chief centers of activity in the city are its many markets. The busiest of them all is the Iron Market, a two-block-long area that got its name not

Words to Understand in This Chapter

mansion—a large, impressive house.
shantytown—a poor area in a city where people live close together in small, loosely constructed homes made typically of rough metal.

A hillside shantytown in Port-au-Prince.

from what is sold there but from the elaborate ironwork on the fronts of many of the buildings in the area. Early in the morning, women arrive in the market. Many of them carry their wares in wicker baskets balanced on their heads. In this and other markets, visitors can find all manner of fresh produce, plus staples like breads, meats, and fish.

CAP-HAÏTIEN

Cap-Haïtien is located along the beautiful Atlantic coast of Haiti's northern plain, within view of the Massif du Nord mountain range. A seaport, Cap-

Haïtien was once called "the Paris of the Antilles" because of its beauty and the culture that had developed there. The present-day city was founded as Cap-Français by the French in 1670.

With a population of about 190,000 people, Cap-Haïtien is less than one-tenth the size of Port-au-Prince. The city's central square, the Place d'Armes, features the city hall and a large cathedral.

As much as any city in Haiti, Cap-Haïtien has been a tourist spot. This is due in part to the nearby Citadelle Laferriere, a huge fortress built in the early 1800s by King Henri Christophe, who ruled the northern part of Haiti at the time. With walls 25 feet (8 meters) thick and up to 130 feet (40 meters) high, it was designed to hold the thousands of soldiers the king felt he needed in case of a French invasion. Located atop a nearby mountain, the castle is now a tourist destination.

JACMEL

About 25 miles (40 km) south of Port-au-Prince, on the southern coast, lies Jacmel, a city of about 40,000 residents. Founded in 1689, the city was once the center of Haiti's coffee export business.

Today, Jacmel is promoting itself as a tourist destination. It features beautiful beaches and 19th-century architecture that recalls the French Quarter of New Orleans. Many of the most attractive structures were once the mansions of Jacmel's wealthy coffee growers. Modern Jacmel still boasts numerous coffeehouses—reminders of its commercial past. It is also home to many members of Jamaica's artistic community, who are drawn by Jacmel's scenic locale as well as its leisurely pace.

GONAÏVES

Along the Gulf of Gonâve, north of Port-au-Prince, lies another important Haitian seaport, Gonaïves. It is home to about 300,000 people, according to Haiti's 2011 census.

In addition to its modern role as a small commercial center and export point for such products as coffee and bananas, Gonaïves has historical significance. It is known as the place where, in 1804, Haiti's independence from France was proclaimed—launching the Caribbean land on the turbulent and troubled journey into nationhood that continues to this day.

 TEXT-DEPENDENT QUESTIONS

1. What does the name Port-au-Prince mean? Why did the city receive this name?
2. What fortress in Cap-Haïtien was built to defend the city from a French invasion?

Haiti is a country of contrasts, and this is reflected in its festivals and observances. Some are purely patriotic. Others are religious—often reflecting the complex, intertwined relationship between the Catholic faith and vodun, or voodoo.

January

On January 1, Haitians celebrate not just **New Year's**, but **Independence Day** as well. This commemorates the day in 1804 when Jean-Jacques Dessalines, a former slave, proclaimed Haiti's independence. People wear their best clothes and enjoy an elaborate meal. Formal marches take place in the capital city of Port-au-Prince. The following day, January 2, is **Ancestors' Day** or **Heroes of the Independence Day**.

Epiphany, observed on January 6, is a Christian celebration commemorating the visit of the Magi, or three kings, to the baby Jesus.

February

Haitians host a huge **Mardi Gras** party on the day before Ash Wednesday, the beginning of the Christian season of Lent. (The exact dates change each year.) A blend of Christian, old African, and vodun traditions, Haiti's Mardi Gras serves as a last chance to celebrate before Lent's 40 days of reflection, penance, and fasting. The party features parades with floats and costumed and painted revelers.

Following the Mardi Gras carnival are **Rara** marches, held every weekend during Lent. Brightly clothed bands from the vodun societies appear in the streets of cities and towns, performing music, doing tricks, and dancing for small donations.

March

The Lenten season leads into the Christian celebrations of **Good Friday** and **Easter**, the dates of which vary from year to year. Haitian Christians spend time with family and attend church services.

After Easter comes the **Spring Festival**, another time of singing, dancing, and parades, but not nearly as colorful as Mardi Gras.

May

May 1: **Agriculture and Labor Day**
May 18: **Flag and University Day**
May 22: **National Sovereignty Day**, dedicated to the head of state and to Haiti's culture.

June

June 22: **Presidents Day**

July

On July 16 the tiny town of Ville-Bonheur is the site of a famous observance known as **Sant d'Eau** or **Vyej Mirak** (Creole for "Virgin of Miracles"). Thousands of Roman Catholics and practitioners of vodun travel to Ville-Bonheur to gather under a waterfall where the Virgin Mary is said to have appeared in the 19th century. There the pilgrims wash away their bad luck.

August

The **Assumption**, observed on August 15, is a Catholic feast commemorating the taking up of Mary, the mother of Jesus Christ, into heaven.

October

On October 17, Haitians mark the anniversary of the death of **Jean-Jacques Dessalines**, remembering this revolutionary who became emperor in 1805.

November

On **All Saints' Day** (November 1) and **All Souls' Day** (November 2), Haitian Catholics honor the saints and pray for the souls of the faithful departed, respectively.

November 18 is celebrated in Haiti as **Battle of Vertieres Day** or **Armed Forces Day**. This commemorates the Haitian victory over the French in 1803.

Around November 25, Haitians observe **Manger-Yam**, a festival celebrating the yam harvest. Singing, dancing, and a feast make the day special.

December

Discovery Day (December 5) commemorates Columbus's landing on the north coast of Hispaniola in 1492.

Like Christians everywhere, Haitians celebrate **Christmas** on December 25.

Griot (Fried Pork)

3 lbs shoulder of pork, cut into 1-to-2-inch cubes
1/2 cup chopped shallots
1 cup bitter orange juice
Salt, pepper, and hot pepper to taste
1 tsp thyme
1 large onion, chopped
1/2 cup vegetable oil

Directions:

1. Put all ingredients except the oil in a large pot and marinate overnight in the refrigerator.
2. Place the pork and marinade on the stove, add water to cover all ingredients, and boil on medium heat for 45 minutes.
3. Once cooked, drain the mixture, add oil, and fry the pork in the pot until brown and crusty on the outside but tender on the inside.

Soup du Haiti

1 pound cubed beef
2 tbsp seasoned salt
1 package fresh spinach, rinsed and torn
2 limes, cut in halves
2 sweet potatoes, chopped
1 boniata (a root vegetable similar to a sweet potato; has red skin and white flesh), chopped
2 potatoes, chopped
1 malanga, chopped
1 green pepper, sliced
3 carrots, chopped
2 onions, sliced
1 tsp thyme
1 tsp parsley
Scallions
3 tbsp tomato paste
Salt, black pepper, and hot pepper to taste

Directions:

1. Rinse meat with hot water and lemon juice.
2. Rub meat with seasoned salt and refrigerate for two hours.
3. Combine meat and spinach in 2 quarts of water and cook about an hour until the meat is tender.
4. Add remaining ingredients and cook an additional 20 minutes or until the potatoes are cooked.

Chicken in Sauce *(Poule en Sauce)*
1 lb chicken
1 tbsp lemon juice or vinegar
1 tbsp parsley
1 tbsp thyme
2 crushed garlic cloves
2 tbsp seasoned salt
2 tbsp oil

Directions:
1. Rub chicken with lemon juice or vinegar and rinse with hot water.
2. Season chicken with parsley, thyme, garlic, and seasoned salt or preferred spices.
3. Marinate in refrigerator 3–4 hours or overnight.
4. Put chicken in a pot, cover with water, and boil for 20 minutes.
5. Prepare sauce (see below).
6. Brown chicken in 2 tbsp oil.
7. Simmer chicken in sauce for 10–15 minutes.

Sauce
1 small onion, sliced
1/2 cup red or green peppers
1 tsp oil
1 cup water
1 1/2 tbsp tomato paste
1 garlic clove
Salt, black pepper, or hot pepper to taste

Directions:
1. Sauté onions and peppers in oil for 1 minute.
2. Add water, bring to a boil, then add remaining ingredients. Stir and simmer sauce on low heat.

Fried Plantain
3 green plantains
Cooking oil
Salt

Directions:
1. Place oil in a skillet over medium-high heat.
2. Sauté half-inch plantain slices until they begin to brown.
3. Remove the plantain and drain on paper towels.
4. Use the bottom of a cup to flatten the plantains.
5. Press to half their size.
6. Sauté once again until golden brown.
7. Remove and use paper towels to absorb excess oil. Sprinkle salt on fried plantain.

Amerindian—a term for the indigenous peoples of North, Central, and South America, including the Caribbean islands, before the arrival of Europeans in the late 15th century.

cay—a low island or reef made from sand or coral.

civil liberty—the right of people to do or say things that are not illegal without being stopped or interrupted by the government.

conquistador—any one of the Spanish leaders of the conquest of the Americas in the 1500s.

Communism—a political system in which all resources, industries, and property are considered to be held in common by all the people, with government as the central authority responsible for controlling all economic and social activity.

coup d'état—the violent overthrow of an existing government by a small group.

deforestation—the action or process of clearing forests.

economic system—the production, distribution, and consumption of goods and services within a country.

ecotourism—a form of tourism in which resorts attempt to minimize the impact of visitors on the local environment, contribute to conserving habitats, and employ local people.

embargo—a government restriction or restraint on commerce, especially an order that prohibits trade with a particular nation.

exploit—to take advantage of something; to use something unfairly.

foreign aid—financial assistance given by one country to another.

free trade—trade based on the unrestricted exchange of goods, with tariffs (taxes) only used to create revenue, not keep out foreign goods.

hurricane—a very powerful and destructive storm, characterized by high winds and significant rainfall, that often occurs in the western Atlantic Ocean and the Caribbean Sea between June and November.

leeward—a side that is sheltered or away from the wind.

mestizo—a person of mixed Amerindian and European (typically Spanish) descent.

offshore banking—a term applied to banking transactions conducted between participants located outside of a country. Such transactions Some Caribbean countries have become known for this practice thanks to their banking laws.

plaza—the central open square at the center of colonial-era cities in Latin America.

plebiscite—a vote by which the people of an entire country express their opinion on a particular government or national policy.

population density—a measurement of the number of people living in a specific area, such a square mile or square kilometer.

pre-Columbian—referring to a time before the 1490s, when Christopher Columbus landed in the Americas.

regime—a period of rule by a particular government, especially one that is considered to be oppressive.

service industry—any business, organization, or profession that does work for a customer, but is not involved in manufacturing.

windward—the side or direction from which the wind is blowing.

Ocean life

Haiti is almost completely surrounded by water. To learn more about the aquatic life around Haiti, create your own ocean diorama. A shoe box will serve as the stage for your ocean scene. Decorate the inside of the box to look like it's underwater. Using colored construction paper, pipe cleaners, and other supplies, create the ocean floor, water, rocks, coral, seaweed—whatever you think you'd find in the waters around Haiti. Then do some research to find out what kinds of aquatic animals live in the area. Find their pictures in old magazines or print them off the Internet. Cut them out and paste them on cardboard. Write each creature's name on the back of the cardboard. Then hang the creatures in your box using tape and thread.

Flashcards

Create flashcards to learn about the historical figures in this book. Put the person's name on one side of the card, then write why he or she is an important part of Haiti's history on the other. Pick a partner and take turns naming the person and detailing his or her place in history. Give yourself a point for each correct answer and keep track of your scores until you've each had a chance to go through all the flashcards.

Make your own puzzle

Using the Internet, find a map of Haiti and print it out. Colored maps look the best. Glue the map onto poster board. Once the glue is thoroughly dried, trim off the excess poster board and cut the map into jigsaw puzzle pieces. Have fun learning about the cities and other features of the map as you put your puzzle back together.

Celebrate Mardi Gras

Mardi Gras is a festival Haitians celebrate each year before Lent. One of the most exciting parts of Mardi Gras is having the chance to dress up in wild costumes. Create your own festive Mardi Gras mask using card-stock paper about the size of your face, markers or crayons, scissors, a stapler, and a one-foot piece of elastic. Cut the paper in the shape you'd like and cut out the eyeholes. Staple one end of the elastic onto the back of the paper near one edge. Determine how much elastic it will take to fit on your head. Trim the elastic so the mask will fit correctly. Staple the remaining side of the elastic to the other side of the mask. Use your imagination to decorate the mask. You can use glitter or other fun, flashy materials.

PROJECT AND REPORT IDEAS

Glossary word find

On a plain piece of paper, create a word find for your friends and classmates. Your page should be able to fit 20 letters across and 20 letters down. Using a pencil and a ruler, lightly make 20 rows from left to right. When complete, do the same going up and down. Then put the glossary terms in the grid you've created, one letter to one box. Once all the glossary terms are on the grid, fill in the rest of the grid with random letters. When your grid is full, make copies and challenge your friends and classmates to find the glossary terms.

Create a Haiti resource page on the Web

Surf the Internet and find websites related to Haiti. Choose the most interesting ones and compile a list. Your class can put the links on its own Web page for others to use. Make sure to write a few sentences about each website so people know what type of information it contains.

Find out more

Write a one-page report on any of the following:

- An animal that calls Haiti home. Talk about what it looks like, where it can be found, what it eats, and other details you find interesting.
- The history of vodun (voodoo).
- Who was Jean-Jacques Dessalines and why is he an important figure in Haiti's history? What characteristics do you think he possessed?
- When did Christopher Columbus land in Haiti? What do you imagine the country was like when he landed? How and why do you think it has changed?
- What part does the topography of Haiti play in the country's economy? Does it limit the types of jobs Haitians can have? What part does it play in where people live?
- How is sugarcane grown and what products are made from it? What products do you use that may be made from sugarcane?
- Sisal is one of Haiti's chief agricultural products. What is it? How is it produced? What is it used for?

pre-1492	A succession of Indian tribes lives on the land that is now Haiti; the Arawak Indians are living there when Europeans first arrive.
1492	Columbus's expedition arrives in the West Indies, and one of the ships, the *Santa María*, runs aground off the northern coast of the island of Hispaniola, near the present-day city of Cap-Haïtien.
early 1500s	Spanish settlers flock to Hispaniola; the Indian population is enslaved or killed; African slaves are brought to the island.
1697	The Treaty of Ryswick gives France control of the land that is now Haiti; Spain retains control of the land that is now the Dominican Republic.
1791	Slaves and mulattoes rise up against the European minority in a revolt led by Toussaint-Louverture.
1802	Napoleon sends more troops to battle the Haitians; after early success, the French army is devastated by yellow fever, and the rebels reclaim their land.
1804	General Jean-Jacques Dessalines, leader of the Haitian rebels, declares the country's independence on January 1; he proclaims himself emperor.
1806	Dessalines is assassinated.
1807–20	Civil war divides the country north and south, until Jean-Pierre Boyer reunites Haiti as one nation.
1821	Boyer invades Santo Domingo after it declares its independence from Spain; Haiti will control the entire island until 1844.
1844–1913	A total of 32 different men rule Haiti.
1915	Woodrow Wilson, the U.S. president, sends troops to Haiti to restore order.
1934	The United States withdraws from Haiti; Aimé Césaire launches the Négritude movement in Paris.
1957	François Duvalier wins election to the presidency.
1964	Duvalier declares himself president-for-life.
1971	Duvalier dies in office after naming his 19-year-old son, Jean-Claude, to succeed him.
1986	A revolt forces Jean-Claude Duvalier to leave the country; General Henri Namphy takes control.
1990	Jean-Bertrand Aristide is elected president.

1991	Aristide is overthrown by the military, leading to an international trade embargo that plunges Haiti even deeper into poverty.
1994	On September 18, the United States, acting on a mandate from the United Nations Security Council, dispatches troops to invade Haiti; while the forces are en route, Haiti's military rulers agree to step aside and let Aristide return to power; U.S. and, later, United Nations peacekeepers maintain order in Haiti.
1995	René Préval is elected president.
1998	The U.N. peacekeeping force pulls out of Haiti.
2000	Aristide is once again elected president; his Lavalas Family Party wins large majorities in Haiti's legislature, but accusations of voter fraud are widespread.
2001	A coup attempt in December fails.
2002	Pro-government groups commit acts of violence and murder against opponents of Aristide; amid increasing civil unrest, critics call for Aristide to resign, but he refuses.
2004	National unrest overshadows celebrations of the 200th anniversary of Haiti's independence in January; on February 29, President Aristide leaves Haiti for exile in South Africa, and Boniface Alexandre is sworn in as interim president.
2006	National elections are held, and René Préval is elected president of Haiti.
2007	Venezuela's Hugo Chavez agrees to invest in new power plants and an oil refinery to be built in Haiti.
2008	Haitians, angry over the high cost of food, riot in Port-au-Prince.
2010	In January, a powerful earthquake devastates Haiti, killing more than 150,000 people.
2011	In May, Michel Martelly is sworn in as Haiti's president.
2014	Cap-Haïtien and other cities in northern Haiti suffer serious flooding in November, leaving more than 12 people dead and thousands homeless.
2015	Anti-government protests continue against high food and fuel prices.

Bartell, Jim. *Haiti*. Minneapolis: Bellwether Media, 2012.

Clammer, Paul, and Michael Grosberg. *Dominican Republic and Haiti*. Oakland, Calif.: Lonely Planet, 2011.

Higate, Paul, and Marsha Henry. *Insecure Spaces: Peacekeeping in Liberia, Kosovo and Haiti*. London: Zed Books, 2008.

Keen, Benjamin, and Keith Haynes. *A History of Latin America*. Boston: Wadsworth Cengage Learning, 2013.

Palmié, Stephan, and Francisco A. Scarano, editors. *The Caribbean: A History of the Region and its Peoples*. Chicago: University of Chicago Press, 2011.

Travel Information

http://www.worldtravelguide.net/country/112/country_guide/Caribbean/Haiti.html
http://www.state.gov/r/pa/ei/bgn/1982.htm

History and Geography

http://www.hartford-hwp.com/archives/43a/
http://news.bbc.co.uk/1/hi/world/americas/country_profiles/1202772.stm
http://geography.about.com/library/cia/blchaiti.htm

Economic and Political Information

https://www.cia.gov/library/publications/the-world-factbook/geos/ha.html
http://www.politicalresources.net/haiti.htm
http://www.haiti.org

Embassy of the Republic of Haiti
2311 Massachusetts Ave., NW
Washington, DC 20008
Phone: 202-332-4090
Fax: 202-745-7215
Website: www.haiti.org
Email: amb.washington@diplomatie.ht

U.S. Embassy in Haiti
Tabarre 41
Route de Tabarre
Port-au-Prince, Haiti
Phone: 011-509-2229-8000
Web site: http://haiti.usembassy.gov

Haitian Consulate in New York
815 Second Ave.
New York, NY 10017
Phone: 212-697-9767
Fax: 212-681-6991
Website: www.haitianconsulate-nyc.org
Email: cg.newyork@diplomatie.ht

Arawak Indians, 17, 18
Aristide, Jean-Bertrand, 23, 24, 25
Artibonite River, 12
Atlantic Ocean, 10
Avril, Prosper, 23

Bonaparte, Napoleon, 20
Boyer, Jean-Pierre, 20–21

Cap-Haïtien, 17, 25, 47–48
Caribbean Sea, 10
Césaire, Aimé, 42
Chavez, Hugo, 32, 33
Christophe, Henri, 20, 48
Creole language, 37, 38
Columbus, Bartholomew, 18
Columbus, Christopher, 9, 14, 17–18
Cuba, 9, 10, 18, 28

Depestre, René, 42
Dessalines, Jean-Jacques, 20
Dominican Republic, 10, 12, 17, 18, 21, 28, 37, 42
Duvalier, François ("Papa Doc"), 21–22
Duvalier, Jean-Claude ("Baby Doc"), 22

France, 19, 20

French language, 37–38
French Revolution, 19–20

Gonaïves, 25, 49
Greater Antilles, 9
Gulf of Gonâve, 10, 12, 45

Haiti
    and 2010 earthquake, 9, 15
    economy of, 27–33
    geography and climate of, 9–15
    health problems in, 36–37
    history of, 9, 17–25, 27, 39–41, 45, 46, 47–49
    people and culture of, 35–43
    poverty in, 27–28, 35, 36, 37, 41
Hispaniola Island, 9, 10, 14, 17, 18, 20
Hurricane Flora, 14
Hurricane Georges, 14

Isle de la Gonâve, 10

Jacmel, 48
Jamaica, 9

La Navidad settlement, 18
Lavalas Family Party, 24, 25

Martinique, 42
Massif de la Hotte, 11
Massif de la Selle, 11
Massif du Nord, 10, 47
Mexico, 18
Montagnes Noires, 10

Namphy, Henri, 22, 23
Négritude movement, 42
Nicaragua, 28

Organization of American States (OAS), 23

Peru, 18
Pétion, Alexandre, 20
Port-au-Prince, 10, 14, 25, 45–47
Préval, René, 24, 25, 32, 33
Puerto Rico, 9

Roman Catholic Church, 23, 36, 39

Saint Domingue (colony of France), 19–20, 27, 46
    See also Haiti, history of
Santa María, 17
Santo Domingo, 19
slavery, 18, 19, 20, 35, 37–38, 39, 41

Spain, 9, 17, 18, 19, 20, 21

Tontons Macoutes, 22
Tortue Island, 19
Toussaint-Louverture, 20
Treaty of Ryswick, 19

United Nations, 23, 24
United States, 14, 21, 23–24, 37, 42
University of Haiti, 36

Venezuela, 32, 33

vodun (voodoo), 39–41

West Indies, 9, 17
Wilson, Woodrow, 21
Windward Passage, 10
World War I, 21

Page
1:   used under license from Shutterstock, Inc.
2:   © OTTN Publishing
3:   © OTTN Publishing
7:   Tony Arruza/Corbis
8:   U.S. Navy Photo
9:   Carl & Ann Purcell/Corbis
11: Bettmann/Corbis
16: United Nations photo
17: United Nations photo
22: Hulton/Archive/Getty Images
24: United Nations photo
25: United Nations photo
26: United Nations photo
27: United Nations photo
29: United Nations photo
32: United Nations photo
34: Paul A. Souders/Corbis
35: Philip Gould/Corbis
38: AFP/Corbis
40: Nicolas Sapieha/Art Resource, NY
42: Arindambanerjee / Shutterstock.com
44: Arindambanerjee / Shutterstock.com
45: Danny Alvarez / Shutterstock.com
47: United Nations photo

CONTRIBUTORS

Senior Consulting Editor **James D. Henderson** is professor of
international studies at Coastal Carolina University. He is the
author of *Conservative Thought in Twentieth Century Latin America:
The Ideals of Laureano Gómez* (1988; Spanish edition *Las ideas de
Laureano Gómez* published in 1985); *When Colombia Bled: A History
of the Violence in Tolima* (1985; Spanish edition *Cuando Colombia se
desangró, una historia de la Violencia en metrópoli y provincia*, 1984);
and coauthor of *A Reference Guide to Latin American History* (2000)
and *Ten Notable Women of Latin America* (1978).

    Mr. Henderson earned a bachelor's degree in history from Centenary College of
Louisiana, and a master's degree in history from the University of Arizona. He then
spent three years in the Peace Corps, serving in Colombia, before earning his doctorate
in Latin American history in 1972 at Texas Christian University.

Bob Temple is the president of Red Line Editorial, Inc., an editorial services firm based
in the Minneapolis–St. Paul area. Bob is an award-winning journalist who has enjoyed
a 16-year career in newspapers and online journalism. He is the author of more than 20
nonfiction books for children and young adults, and seven Internet-related titles.